# GEOFFREY TANKARD
## and
## ERIC HARRISON

# PIANOFORTE TECHNIQUE

## ON AN HOUR A DAY

T0078755

Order No: NOV 262558

NOVELLO PUBLISHING LIMITED

## FOREWORD

It may be thought that there are already so many books of technical exercises as to make the production of a new one superfluous. Too many of those available are, however, of limited application. We have often found it necessary to help a pupil, faced with some special technical problem, by writing out exercises during a lesson in order to save him the expense and delay of buying another book; we have decided accordingly to produce under one cover a series of exercises dealing with all the problems with which a pupil is likely to be confronted. We have included a chart which suggests how to allocate with the greatest advantage the time available for practising technique.

It is our sincere hope that this result of our experience will prove useful to other teachers and to students.

Geoffrey Tankard
Eric Harrison

# HINTS ON PRACTISING

1. Learn the hands separately first; try to attain a pure legato and absolute equality of time and tone.
2. Practise the exercises at three different speeds: slow - moderate - fast.
3. Practise them at three levels of tone: *f - mf - p*, and sometimes at different levels between the hands, e.g. L.H. *f* R.H. *p*, etc.
4. If you find transposition confusing, *imagine* the key-signature.
5. Most of the exercises can be played in all keys.
6. Never practice them at a speed beyond your control.
7. Always listen carefully. (If you do this you will never be bored).
8. Many of these exercises can be practised staccato.
9. The fingers may be lifted high in forte practice (say, $\frac{3}{4}$ of an inch from the key surface for *mf*, $\frac{1}{4}$ inch for *p*,) when practicable and comfortable. Commonsense must guide you in this (no two hands are alike, and it is impossible to generalise).
10. When your muscles begin to tire, stop at once. Shake the arm and hand loosely, and after a short rest change the type of exercise.
11. Be as relaxed as is compatible with speed, control and tonal dynamics. Complete relaxation is not possible. Too much tightness hinders velocity and endurance, too much relaxation is 'floppy' and uncontrolled.
12. Use rotary and lateral movements with control and economy, using as much as is required to assist the fingers and no more.
13. Try to prepare (or cover) the key before playing it, and play perpendicularly into the key with the finger movement. This was insisted on by Emil Sauer, Busoni and Pachmann.

## SUGGESTED PRACTICE CHART COVERING 1 HOUR A DAY FOR SIX DAYS

| | MONDAY | TUESDAY | WEDNESDAY | THURSDAY | FRIDAY | SATURDAY |
|---|---|---|---|---|---|---|
| 10 mins. (each group) | Five-finger exercises | Weak fingers (5 mins.) / Part playing (5 mins.) | Scales | Tremolando / Divided hands | Octaves / Double notes | Phrasing / Extensions |
| 10 mins. | Tremolando / Divided hands | Five finger exercises | Arpeggios | Octaves / Double notes | Scales | Repetitions / Leaps |
| 10 mins. | Scales | Phrasing / Broken octaves | Five-finger exercises | Trills | Weak fingers / Part playing | Octaves / Double notes |
| 10 mins. | Tonal gradation / Contractions | Scales | Octaves / Double notes | Five-finger exercises | Arpeggios | Ad lib ★ |
| 10 mins. | Octaves / Double notes | Trills | Tonal gradation / Passing thumb below | Ad lib ★ | Five finger exercises | Scales |
| 10 mins. | Arpeggios | Octaves / Double notes | Repetitions / Leaps | Scales | Tonal gradation / Chords | Five-finger exercises |

★ Ad lib— work at your special weakness.

# SOME RHYTHMIC VARIATIONS ON BASIC PATTERNS

and different patterns in each hand

© 1960 Elkin & Co. Ltd.

E. & Co. 2558

# FIVE FINGER EXERCISES

(N.B. Do not let the hand fall away towards the fifth finger, build up the weaker part of the hand)

## PRELIMINARY

(a) Hand resting on, not squeezing, the sustained silent notes.

(b) Count "up—down—up—down" slowly and evenly.

(c) Play *forte* and raise each finger at least half an inch before striking.

REPEAT with unoccupied fingers resting on key-surfaces, not depressing
LATER, repeat Vivace

Use the modulating pattern (as written in the first exercise) in all subsequent exercises marked *"Mod"*.

etc. to C major

E. & Co. 2558

Though all keys, major, minor, and transition into the next chromatic key above.

**11.** In C, D♭ and E major and minor (legato and staccato)

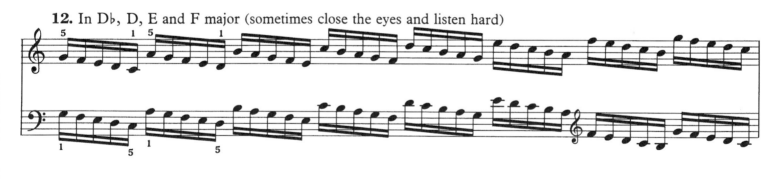

**12.** In D♭, D, E and F major (sometimes close the eyes and listen hard)

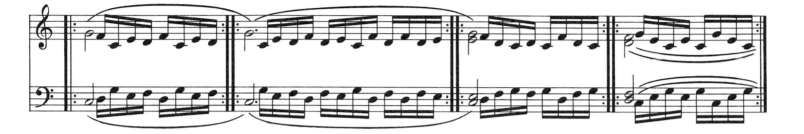

**12 (b).**

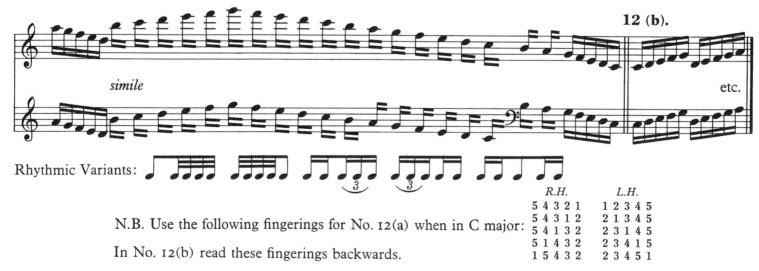

*simile*

*etc.*

Rhythmic Variants:

N.B. Use the following fingerings for No. 12(a) when in C major:

In No. 12(b) read these fingerings backwards.

|  R.H. |  L.H. |
|---|---|
| 5 4 3 2 1 | 1 2 3 4 5 |
| 5 4 3 1 2 | 2 1 3 4 5 |
| 5 4 1 3 2 | 2 3 1 4 5 |
| 5 1 4 3 2 | 2 3 4 1 5 |
| 1 5 4 3 2 | 2 3 4 5 1 |

# PASSING OF THUMB IN SCALE PASSAGES

*Preliminary method of practising Nos.* **1** *to* **5**
Keep the hand still (but wrist NOT stiff), and move the thumb in two planes only,
from the lowest joint—straight down and up to play a note, and straight from side to
side to get over the next note; every movement slow and without a jerk.
*Thereafter,* avoid jerks and twists at any speed.

**1.** (Hands separate)       **2.**       **3.**

**4.** *ten.*       **5.**

**6.** (Hands together)

Scale of C major, two octaves ascending and descending:-

(a) fingered $\begin{smallmatrix}1\,2\,1\,2\,1\,2\\1\,2\,1\,2\,1\,2\end{smallmatrix}$ *etc.*     (i) Similar motion

(b) fingered $\begin{smallmatrix}1\,3\,1\,3\,1\,3\\1\,3\,1\,3\,1\,3\end{smallmatrix}$ *etc.*     (ii) Contrary motion

(c) fingered $\begin{smallmatrix}1\,4\,1\,4\,1\,4\\1\,4\,1\,4\,1\,4\end{smallmatrix}$ *etc.*

**7.** Also in E, etc.

**8.** Also in F♯, etc.

**9.** Also in B♭ minor, etc.

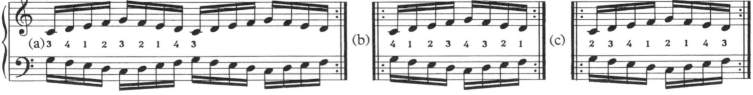

**10.** Also in A, etc.

**11.**

**12.**

**13.** Also in E, etc.

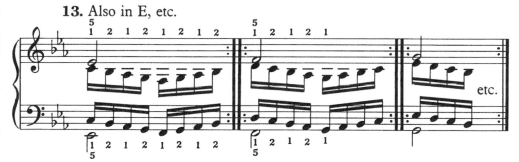

**14.**
Scales of E♭, A♭ and B♭ major with fingering of C major. ★

**15.**

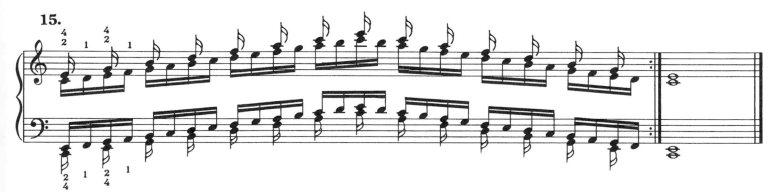

★ This was a favourite exercise of Frederic Lamond's

E. & Co. 2558

**16. Presto**

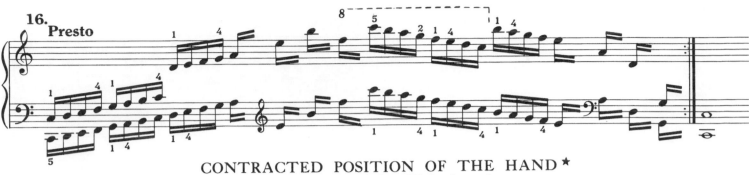

## CONTRACTED POSITION OF THE HAND ★
Left hand an octave below Right throughout

**1.**
**Very clean and clear** (watch the 4th finger)

**2.**

**3.**

**4.**

(★ Favourite exercises of TAUSIG).

# CHORDS

(a) There is a great divergence of style in chord-playing. The essentials are: fingers must be firm; the hand can play light chords, the arm must play heavy ones. Try to feel each finger in a chord, and never hit or slap at the key surfaces.

(b) It is advisable to practise them no shorter than *a staccato of measurable length* rather than staccatissimo. Listen to the inner notes. Develop a harmonic ear.

(c) The fingering 3 or 4 refers to the inner note (1, 2, 5 are always used)

Hands separately at first. Also in contrary motion.

**1.**

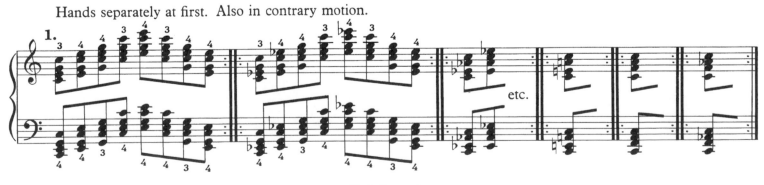

etc. through
the keys, and
in contrary
motion.

**2.** Also in Db, D, Eb, E.

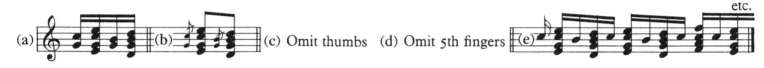

Also in C♯, D, Eb and E. Examples of technique for increasing the clarity of the inner notes:-

etc.

(a)  (b)  (c) Omit thumbs  (d) Omit 5th fingers  (e)

Always decide whether 3rd or 4th finger should be used, then use the right one all the time.

**3.** Use the same modulating pattern as No. 1.

**4.** Same modulating pattern

**5.** Use the same inner-note practise as in No. 2.

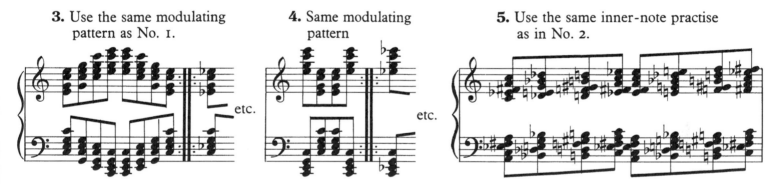

etc.

etc.

**6.**

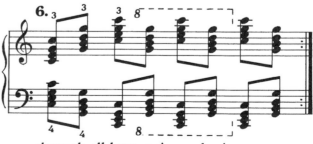

through all keys major and minor.

# BROKEN OCTAVES

**1(a).**  Use a slight controlled rotary action; practise them *p* and *mf* only.

etc. through
the keys.

**1(b).**

etc. as I(a)

**1(c).**

etc.

**1(d).**

etc.

**2.** Not fast; short note light, long note heavy. Also in C minor harmonic, C sharp major and minor.

**3.** Better with 4th fingers on black notes.

**4.** L.H. two octaves below R.H. for the remainder. Fourth fingers on black notes.

**5.**

In all keys, major
and harmonic minor.

**6.** Sometimes close the eyes.

etc. through
the keys.

**7.**

# ARPEGGIOS

**1(a).** Hold long notes, and swing easily and rhythmically without jerking.

**1(b).**

and so on,
through
the keys.

etc. through
the keys.

**2.**
**Not fast;** bridge the gap with control and economy.

Also in D, E, F, G, A and B.

**3.**

and in all
white keys

**4.** Each bar 10 times (rest when tired)
Sustain all notes, with bent fingers (if possible)

etc.

etc.

16

**5.** Also in contrary motion from middle C.

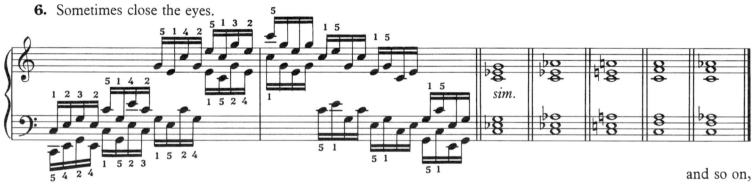

Rhythmic Variants:

**6.** Sometimes close the eyes.

*sim.*

and so on,
through the keys.

**7.**

etc.

**8. Presto**

and in all white keys

# EXTENSIONS and LATERAL EXERCISES
### (*molto legato* throughout)

**1.(a).** Used by Emil Sauer: legato inner notes.

etc. through the keys.

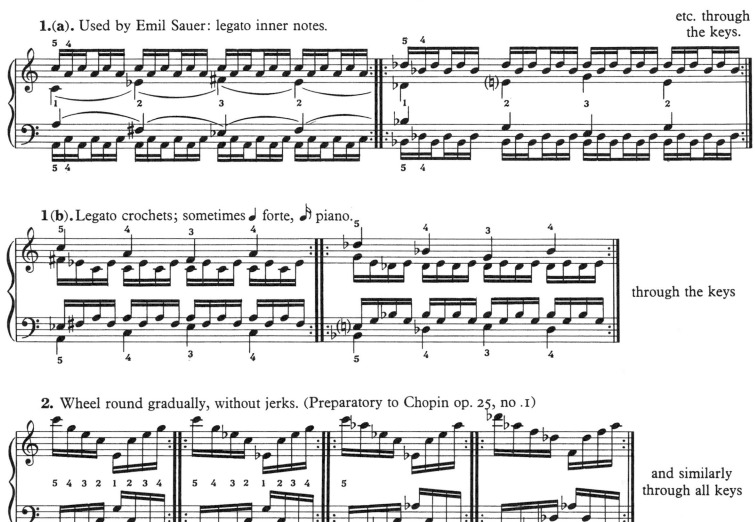

**1(b).** Legato crochets; sometimes ♩ forte, ♪ piano.

through the keys

**2.** Wheel round gradually, without jerks. (Preparatory to Chopin op. 25, no .1)

and similarly through all keys

**3.** (Preparatory to Chopin op. 10, no. 1)

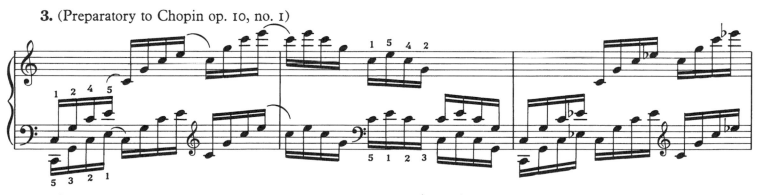

through all keys.

**4.** Do not force, and rest when even a little tired.

etc. through the keys

modulating as in 3 and 4.

and in various keys.

19

**7.** Preparatory to Chopin op. 10, no. 3

ascending two octaves (and descending)

**8.**

In all white keys

**9.** For lateral freedom

**Allegro**

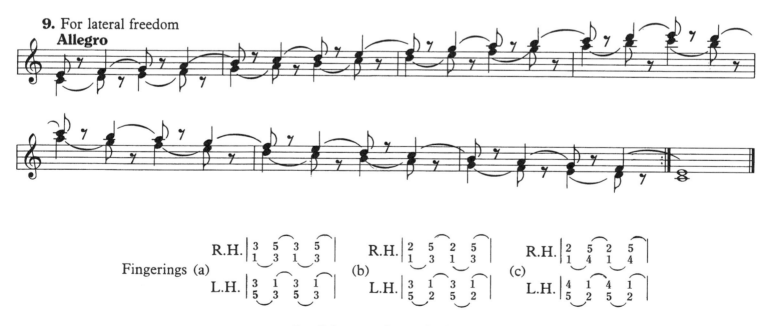

Fingerings (a) R.H. 3 5 3 5 / 1 3 1 3   L.H. 3 1 3 1 / 5 3 5 3   (b) R.H. 2 5 2 5 / 1 3 1 3   L.H. 3 1 3 1 / 5 2 5 2   (c) R.H. 2 5 2 5 / 1 4 1 4   L.H. 4 1 4 1 / 5 2 5 2

In all keys, major and minor

# TRILLS

N.B. Avoid stiff wrists and cramped palms. Trills should be physically pleasurable.
*Never* press, physically or mentally. Use hand knuckles, not elbows.

Also in D, E♭, F♯, A.

The following are different trill positions. They should be practised, after the appropriate preliminaries 2(a) and (b), with all these pairs of fingers, 12, 13, 14, 15, 24, 25, 34, 35, 45.

Then tremolos in various positions of major and minor 3rd., then 4ths., 5ths, etc. and compound tremolos, e.g.

Use fingers *p* level.
Use arms *mf* level.

N.B. Thalberg's favourite fingering for trills:

Try also 13232323 13232323. These are sometimes helpful in very forceful trills.

# OCTAVES

(a) Use a considerable hand (wrist) stroke in slow practice; with increasing speed this movement is reduced.
(b) Always try to relax the underside of the wrist whilst the note is sounding. (See note (b) on chords)
(c) Practise a scale in octaves every day.

**1.**

Variant Rhythm:

etc.

In all keys.

**2.**

In all keys.

**3.** *Preliminary:*

**4.**

Also in G, A♭, A, B♭.

**5.**

Also in D♭, D, E♭, E.

**6.** (a) Legato moderato
(b) Leggiero presto

etc. to          etc. to

**7(a).** *Preliminary:*          *Then:*

etc. through the major and minor keys.

**7(b).**

etc. through the major and minor keys.

**7(c).**

etc. through the major and minor keys.

**8.** Given to Clara Schumann by Frederick Wieck. Sometimes watch the changed notes, sometimes the static.

*Variant*

**9(a).** Use 4th finger on black keys. Sometimes close the eyes. Can also be used on dominant 7ths.

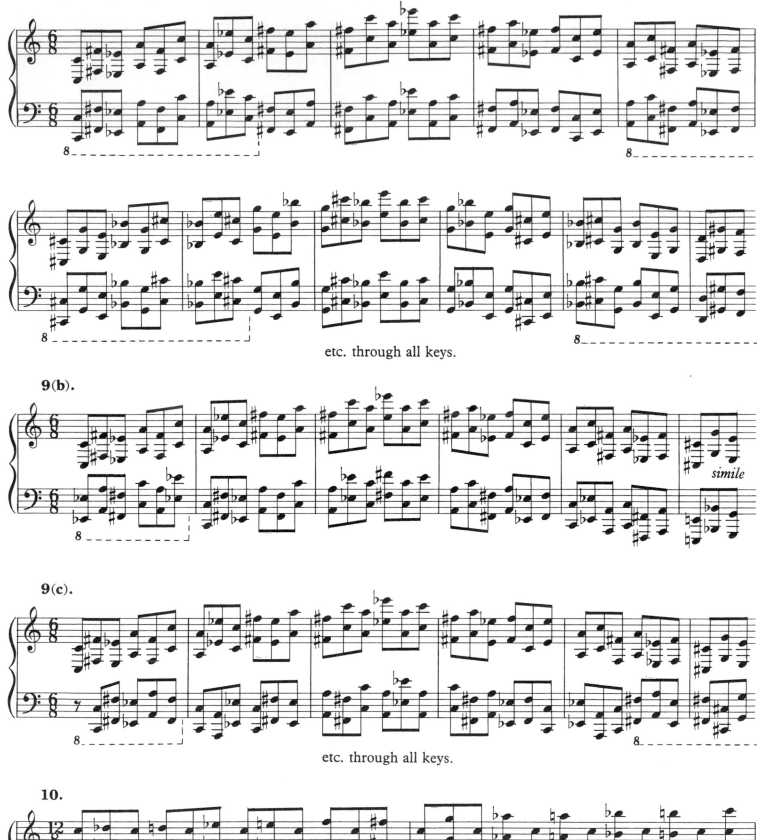

etc. through all keys.

**9(b).**

*simile*

**9(c).**

etc. through all keys.

**10.**

**11.**

etc. through all keys.

**12.**

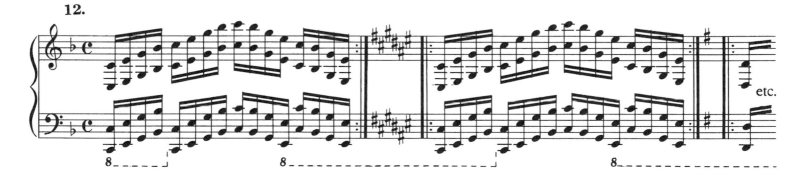

**13.** *Acciaciaturas* ***pp***, *minims* ***ff***

# DOUBLE NOTES

**1(a).**

etc. through
the keys.

**1(b).**

etc.

**1(c).**

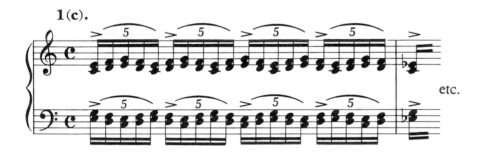

etc.

**1(d).**

etc.

**1(e).**

etc.

**2(a).** Depress sustained note in advance if helpful.

**2(b).**

**2(c).**

**2(d).**

*Variants*

**3(a).**

Also in D, E♭ and E major and C minor harmonic.

**3(b).**

Also in D♭ & A major

**3(c).** *Absolutely legato in all parts* (Walk sideways like a crab)

**3(d).** Godowsky insisted on outer and inner notes being studied separately.

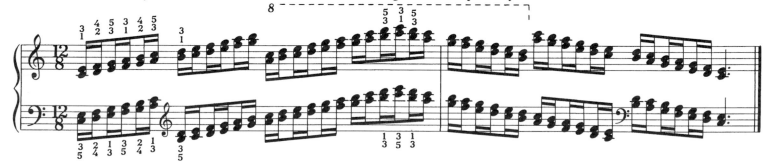

**4.**

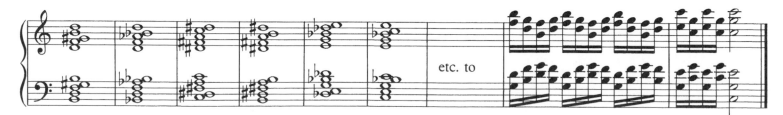

etc. to

*Variant*

**5.**

**6(a).**★ With high strokes, and from surface level.★

etc. to

etc.

**6(b).**★

**7.**★

Also in D, E♭ and E

**8.** *As Legato as possible.*

Also in F, G, A♭.

★ N.B. Make neat changes of position. (Preparation for Schumann Toccata, Brahms Paganini Variations, etc.)

# WEAK FINGERS

N.B. These exercises can be dangerous if practised excessively. Three minutes twice
daily is better than fifteen minutes continuous work, especially for a weak hand.

**1.**

Also in Db, D, Eb, E, F.

**2.**

**3.**

**4(a).**

etc.
through the keys.

**4(b).**

etc.

**5(a).**

etc.

**5(b).**

etc.

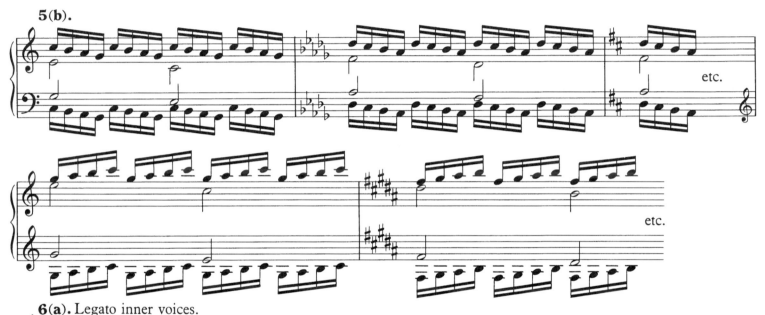

etc.

**6(a).** Legato inner voices.

etc.

**6(b).**

etc.

**6(c).**

etc.

**7(a).**

Also in D, Eb, F

**7(b).**

Also in E, F#, Bb

**8.**
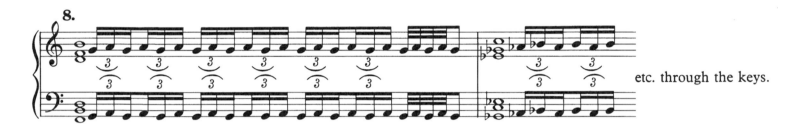
etc. through the keys.

**9.**

etc. through the keys.

**10.**
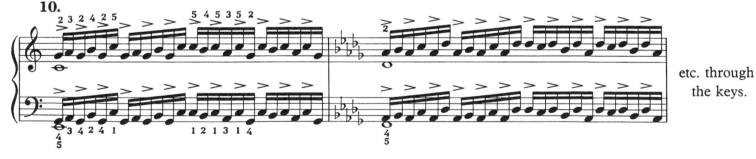
etc. through the keys.

**11.**

In all keys.

E & Co. 2558

# REPETITION

**1.** Strike tied notes silently but forcefully (Level of hand should remain undisturbed)

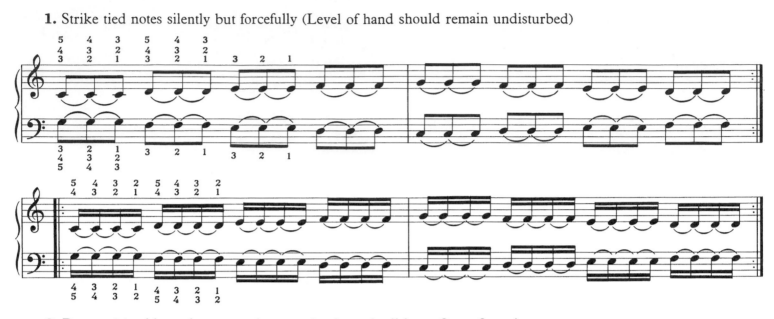

**2.** Repeat (1) without ties, at varying speeds, through all keys. Same fingerings

*N.B.* Make the last note of each group as staccato as the others.

**3.**

etc.
through the keys.

**4(a).**

**4(b).**

**5.**

etc. through the chromatic scale.

**6.**

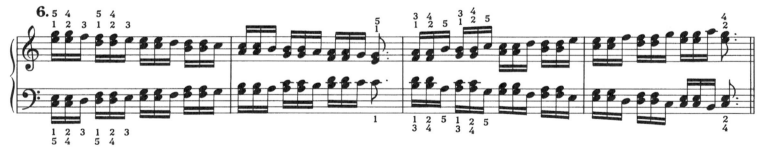

**7.**

# ALTERNATING HANDS

**1.** Sometimes close the eyes. Can be played first as chords until distances are memorised.

**2(a).**

etc. through the keys.

Also in D♭ major and minor

**2(b).**

Also in A♭ and
B major and minor

**3.** Do not employ the thumbs.

etc.    etc.

and so on
through
the keys.

**4(a).**

Also in E major and E♭ minor

38

**4(b).** Right hand over.

Also in
F# major
and G minor

**5(a).**

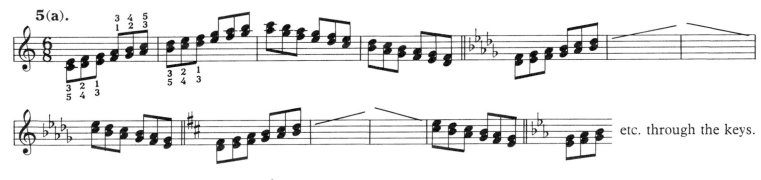

etc. through the keys.

**5(b).**

**6.**

etc. through
the keys.

# TONE GRADATION

*N.B.* Anticipate each sound in your mind's ear before you make it. Tend to *delay* crescendos and diminuendos; never be premature.

Leschetizky used to imagine a kind of "Beaufort Scale" of dynamic strengths; see examples "L.S." in Exercises Nos. 1 & 2

(Use pedal continuously in the crescendo; change as necessary to reduce accumulated resonance during the diminuendo. "Weigh" the key resistance sensitively)

**6.** Crescendo (possible only on first-class pianos) from *ppp* to *fff* through 55 Chords.

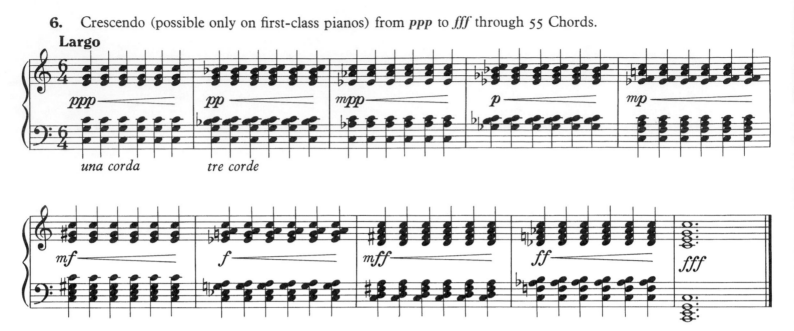

una corda

tre corde

# PHRASING

Lift the hand gracefully on the last note of the phrase.

**1.** **Moderato**

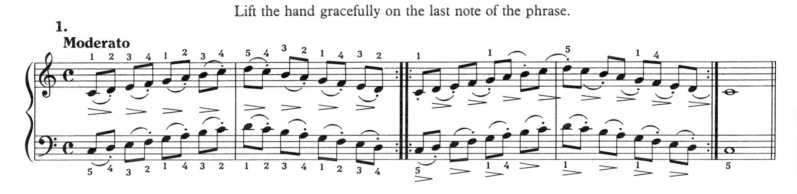

C major fingering

**2.★** **Expressively**

★ Practise the hands separately until the muscular movements are memorised.

**Con espress.**

**3.** Legato and portamento (4th fingers on black notes)

**4.** Combined legato and staccato. Changed notes legato, repeated notes finger-staccato

etc.

etc.

etc.

# APPENDIX

## SUGGESTIONS FOR SCALE PRACTICE

In all keys, major and minor.
Two octaves apart, (for hearing L.H. more clearly)

*Crossing the hands. Right hand over and right hand under. (Also helpful in listening to L.H.)

Two octaves apart.  *sim.*

*Third apart. (Also tenth apart, reversed hands)

*Sixth apart. (Also reversed hands)

* Be careful to keep to the proper fingering.

44

Crossing the hands.

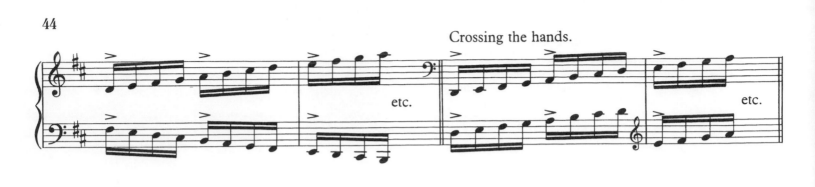

Evenly

*N.B.* Be careful to keep to the proper fingering.

# Intermediate Piano Music

| | | |
|---|---|---|
| **Clifford Benson** | : | Three Pieces for Piano (5 – 6) |
| **Peter Dickinson** | : | Five Diversions (5) |
| **C. S. Lang** | : | Sketches for Piano (3 – 4) |
| **Joan Last** | : | Time for Leisure (4) |
| **Kenneth Leighton** | : | Pieces for Angela (3) |
| **Edward Macdowell** | : | To a Wild Rose (4) |
| **John McCabe** | : | Afternoons and Afterwards (5) |
| **Jean-Philippe Rameau** | : | The Easier Rameau *arranged by Eve Barsham* (4) |
| **Erik Satie** | : | Entertainment (4 – 5) |
| **Franz Schubert** | : | The Easier Schubert *arranged by Eve Barsham* (4) |
| **Cyril Scott** | : | For My Young Friends (3 – 4) |

*Figures indicate the Associated Board grade level*

the indispensable

# GEOFFREY TANKARD

books

---

## FOUNDATIONS OF PIANOFORTE TECHNIQUE
a series of exercises from Grades 2 to 8

---

## PIANOFORTE TECHNIQUE
## ON AN HOUR A DAY
a series of exercises dealing with all the
problems with which a pupil is likely to
be confronted

---

## PIANOFORTE DIPLOMAS & DEGREES
a book intended to help prospective candidates
in preparing for examinations

---

## SPECIMEN ANSWERS
## TO THE QUESTIONS IN
## 'PIANOFORTE DIPLOMAS & DEGREES'

---